THE SUCCESS OF DIVESTITURES IN MERGER ENFORCEMENT: EVIDENCE FROM THE J&J – PFIZER TRANSACTION

I.   Introduction

Under the Hart-Scott-Rodino (HSR) Antitrust Improvements Act of 1976, mergers of sufficient size are subject to review by either the Federal Trade Commission (FTC) or the Department of Justice (DOJ).[1] If a transaction is deemed anticompetitive, the antitrust agencies may attempt to block it or modify the transaction in a manner that alleviates the competitive concern.

An assessment of the success of merger policy can potentially look at two different margins. First, do the antitrust authorities correctly identify which mergers are anticompetitive? Second, conditional on the antitrust agencies obtaining relief, is the remedy sufficient to prevent anticompetitive effects?

Empirical analyses of the success of merger policy have largely focused on the first question. The typical study investigates whether a merger in which the antitrust authorities did not obtain relief led to anticompetitive effects (see Section II). If so, the policy implication is that antitrust enforcement should be stricter. For this to be true, however, antitrust remedies must effectively maintain competition, rather than simply being "pyrrhic victories" (Elzinga, 1969). As such, whether the antitrust agencies obtain effective relief can be just as important as whether they correctly identify anticompetitive mergers.

Nonetheless, few studies consider the effectiveness of the relief obtained by the antitrust authorities. This might be expected if the typical remedy in merger cases blocked the transaction, since there would be no competitive change to analyze. This is not the case, however. Of the 144 mergers challenged by the FTC or DOJ over the period 2003-2007, 51%

---

[1] For 2009, the HSR minimum reporting threshold is $65.2 million (http://www.ftc.gov/os/fedreg/2009/january/090113section7aclaytonact.pdf).

were settled via consent orders, and an additional 13% were restructured after the DOJ informed the parties of its concerns.[2]

The typical remedy in a merger case requires divestiture of the competitive overlap. Since the divested products are sold to firms with little or no presence in the overlap market, this outcome maintains market concentration at the pre-merger level. Divestiture is a particularly attractive remedy since it requires relatively little ongoing regulatory overview (as compared to, say, a conduct remedy that directly regulates price).

Despite being a widely used tool in merger enforcement, there have been few studies of whether antitrust divestitures are successful in preserving the pre-merger level of competition. We help fill this void by conducting a study of Johnson & Johnson's (J&J) $16.6 billion acquisition of Pfizer's consumer health division in 2006. This division contained a large number of well-known brands, including Listerine mouthwash and Sudafed cold medicine. The FTC investigated this transaction. To alleviate antitrust concern the merging parties divested six brands (see Section III for background on the transaction).

The J&J – Pfizer divestitures are interesting cases to study for several reasons. First, they are examples of entire lines of business being divested. The FTC frequently follows this practice based, in part, on a FTC Bureau of Competition study that found such divestitures are more successful than divestitures of selected assets (FTC, 1999).[3] In addition, an "up front" buyer was chosen prior to the FTC's acceptance of the proposed consent agreement for public comment. This practice has also become a frequent feature of antitrust divestitures (Baer and Redcay, 2001).

---

[2] HSR annual reports for fiscal years 2003-2007. Available at http://www.ftc.gov/bc/anncompreports.shtm. Only 9% of challenged mergers were litigated, with the remaining 28% abandoned by the parties.

[3] The FTC's divestiture policy is articulated in its "Frequently Asked Questions about Merger Consent Order Provisions," available at http://www.ftc.gov/bc/mergerfaq.shtm. See also, "Statement of the Federal Trade Commission's Bureau of Competition on Negotiating Merger Remedies," available at http://www.ftc.gov/bc/bestpractices/bestpractices030401.shtm.

The J&J – Pfizer transaction is a merger of two conglomerates. This setting commonly results in divestitures. The overlap that raises competitive concern often comprises a small portion of such deals, and the overlap products are often not the primary rationale for the transaction. Negotiating a divestiture with the antitrust authorities can be particularly efficient in such settings, since the time cost of delaying the entire transaction to litigate the merger can be high relative to the cost of divesting the (fairly minor) overlaps. This would appear to be the case in the J&J – Pfizer matter, where the divested brands comprise approximately 5% of the total value of the transaction.

We analyze the impact of the J&J – Pfizer divestitures on several commonly employed sales metrics: dollar and volume sales, retail distribution, and price. A standard "before-after" estimator is used to measure each brand's post-divestiture change. In addition, we consider a "difference in difference" estimator that measures the post-divestiture change relative to a control group of other brands in the same product category.

For three of the brands, their post-divestiture performance is similar to their pre-divestiture performance, while the remainder underwent changes that do not appear to be divestiture related. However, the obtained results are sensitive to the maintained assumption regarding each brand's counterfactual performance had the divestitures not taken place. Moreover, significant heterogeneity across the control group leads to imprecise estimates. Overall, however, the results are consistent with the view that the divestitures maintained the pre-transaction level of competition.

The layout of the paper is as follows. Section II reviews the previous literature. Section III provides additional background on the J&J – Pfizer transaction. The data is described in Section IV. Section V details the estimation methodology. Results are presented in Section VI and Section VII concludes.

II.   Literature Review

Research analyzing the success of merger policy has largely focused on consummated mergers. Retrospective studies have been undertaken in numerous industries to test whether mergers were anticompetitive.[4] Several studies have sought to determine whether claimed efficiencies from mergers were actually realized (Kaplan, 2000; Pesendorfer, 2003; Breen, 2004).

Far fewer studies have analyzed the impact of antitrust divestitures. Elzinga (1969) considers 39 cases filed between 1954 and 1960 where relief was obtained by 1965 (not all of which involved a divestiture). Elzinga determines that in 29 cases the obtained relief was either unsuccessful or deficient. Reasons include the fact that no divestitures were offered, only partial assets were sold, and deficiencies with the buyer of the asset. Rogowsky (1986) uses a similar approach to Elzinga and analyzes 104 cases that occurred from 1968-1980 where relief was achieved by 1981 (again, not all of the cases involved a divestiture). When timeliness is included as a success criterion, in most cases the obtained relief was deemed unsuccessful or deficient.

In response to the limited early success of antitrust remedies, the HSR Act of 1976 was passed. The HSR Act gave the antitrust agencies authority to analyze a merger prior to consummation. It allowed the agencies to negotiate and implement antitrust relief, such as divestitures, far more quickly.

Only a few papers analyze the impact of divestitures since the HSR Act was passed. Cotterill et al. (1999) study two local markets in Connecticut to determine the impact of divestitures related to Royal Ahold's supermarket acquisition of Stop & Shop in 1996. They find that price initially fell after the divestitures, but subsequently trended back up. Lacking pre-

---

[4] For surveys, see Pautler (2003), Whinston (2006), Hunter et al. (2008), and Weinberg (2008). Recently examined industries include hospitals (Vita and Sacher, 2001; Haas-Wilson and Garmon, 2009), oil (Hastings and Gilbert, 2005; Simpson and Taylor, 2008), airlines (Peters, 2006), and consumer products (Ashenfelter and Hosken, 2008).

divestiture data and prices for competing stores, Cotterill et al. do not attempt to control for the counterfactual to the divestiture. Rogers and Hollinger (2004) analyze two oil mergers in 1984 (Texaco-Getty Oil and Socal-Gulf Oil). They find that prices did not rise post-merger, suggesting that the divestitures were successful. Burke (1998) and Piloff (2002) examine the performance of divested bank branches associated with mergers that occurred between 1985-1992 and 1989-1999, respectively. Burke finds that almost all the divested branches remained viable and did not lose (and often gained) market share. Consequently, he concludes divestitures are effective in bank mergers. Piloff finds that, after an initial "runoff period" during which bank deposits decline, divested branches perform as well as other branches.

In 1999, the FTC's Bureau of Competition published a study that reviewed the Commission's divestiture orders during the period 1990 through 1994.[5] This study focused on the asset divestiture process and largely relied on qualitative information gathered from interviews with the buyers of divested assets. The Bureau's divestiture study found that approximately 75% of the divestures remained in operation at the time of the interview. While existence is a necessary condition for a divestiture to be successful, it is insufficient to determine whether the divestiture maintained competition at the pre-merger level. A central conclusion of the Bureau's divestiture study is that entire lines of business should be divested, rather than select assets, since such divestitures have a much higher success rate. This recommendation has been incorporated into many FTC divestiture orders.[6]

Since the Bureau's divestiture study was published, we are unaware of a study in the U.S. that analyzes merger-related divestitures.[7] Indeed, a 2002 GAO report notes that the FTC has not measured the impact of its divestitures since implementing policy changes summarized in the

---

[5] The divestiture study is available at http://www.ftc.gov/os/1999/08/divestiture.pdf.

[6] See the citations in footnote 3 for a discussion of the FTC's divestiture policy.

[7] Soetevent et al. (2008) analyze the impact of a forced divestiture of gas stations in the Netherlands. This is of limited relevance to U.S. antitrust divestiture policy.

1999 divestiture study, and recommends such analysis be undertaken. In an effort to assess the success of the FTC's current divesture policy, we analyze the performance of the six brands divested in the J&J – Pfizer transaction.

III.   Transaction Background

In June 2006, Pfizer reached an agreement with J&J to sell its consumer health division for $16.6 billion.[8] Pfizer's division had sales of $3.9 billion, and contained a wide range of well-known brands including Listerine mouthwash and Sudafed cold medicine. The vast majority of the proposed transaction did not involve categories in which both companies had a significant presence. There were a few instances, however, where the transaction raised possible antitrust concern. To alleviate such concern, in October 2006 the parties agreed to sell five brands to Chattem for $410 million, and the Zantac brand to Boehringer Ingelheim for $510 million.[9] These divestitures represent slightly more than 5% of the value of the transaction.

On December 12, 2006, the FTC announced it was challenging the terms of the proposed acquisition.[10] The FTC alleged the transaction would reduce competition in the U.S. markets for over-the-counter (OTC) H2-blockers, hydrocortisone anti-itch products, nighttime sleep aids, and diaper rash treatments. The FTC simultaneously announced that J&J and Pfizer had agreed to settle the Commission's charges by divesting a brand in each of these categories (which the companies had previously stated they were selling to Chattem and Boehringer Ingelheim).[11] The FTC consent agreement required all assets related to these brands be divested. The J&J – Pfizer

---

[8] "J&J to buy Pfizer's Consumer Health Division for $16.6 billion," USA Today, June 26, 2006.

[9] "Boehringer to Buy Pfizer's Zantac for $509.5 Million," Bloomberg, October 12, 2006. "Chattem to Buy J&J, Pfizer brands for $410 million," San Diego Tribune, October 6, 2006. These transactions were made contingent on J&J's acquisition of Pfizer's consumer health division.

[10] The FTC's complaint and "Aid to Public Comment" are available at http://www.ftc.gov/os/caselist/0610220/0610220.shtm.

[11] As discussed below, the parties divested two other brands, Kaopectate and ACT, in anticipation of possible competitive concerns. We treat these brands as part of the divestiture.

transaction was subsequently consummated on December 20, 2006. The divestitures to Chattem and Boehringer Ingelheim closed approximately two weeks later.[12]

In its "Aid to Public Comment," the FTC explained why it believed Boehringer Ingelheim was a qualified acquirer of the Zantac business. Boehringer Ingelheim manufactured a variety of prescription pharmaceuticals and OTC drugs such as Dulcolax. It was part of the Boehringer Ingelheim Group, a leading worldwide pharmaceutical manufacturer and the eighth largest manufacturer and marketer of OTC health care products worldwide. Boehringer Ingelheim had an existing distribution network that sold products through the same sales channels as Zantac. Lastly, Boehringer Ingelheim had a prior record of successful acquisitions.

The FTC believed that Chattem was a well-qualified acquirer for similar reasons. The Commission noted that Chattem was a leading manufacturer and marketer of a broad portfolio of OTC health care products, toiletries, and dietary supplements, including brands such as Icy Hot and Gold Bond. In addition, Chattem had existing relationships with major retailers and a record of successful prior acquisitions.

Below, we provide a brief overview of the divested brands, which is drawn from the FTC's "Aid to Public Comment."

H2-Blockers

The FTC alleged the transaction would reduce competition in the market for OTC H2-blockers, a class of drugs used for the prevention and relief of heartburn associated with acid indigestion. At the time of the divestiture, this category had sales of $360 million in the U.S., with Pfizer's Zantac and J&J's Pepcid having a combined share of over 70%. All assets related to Zantac were divested to Boehringer Ingelheim.

---

[12] The week beginning January 7, 2007, corresponds to the start of the post-divestiture period in our empirical analysis.

Hydrocortisones

The FTC alleged the transaction would reduce competition in the market for OTC hydrocortisone anti-itch products, which are used for the topical treatment of minor skin irritations, itching, and rashes. At the time of the divestiture, this category had sales of $120 million in the U.S., with Pfizer's Cortizone and J&J's Cortaid having a combined share of over 55%. All assets related to Cortizone were divested to Chattem.

Sleep Aids

The FTC alleged the transaction would reduce competition in the market for OTC nighttime sleep aids, which are used for the relief of occasional sleeplessness. At the time of the divestiture, this category had sales of $100 million in the U.S., with Pfizer's Unisom and J&J's Simply Sleep having a combined share of over 45%. All assets related to Unisom were divested to Chattem.

Diaper Rash Treatments

The FTC alleged the transaction would reduce competition in the market for OTC diaper rash treatments. At the time of the divestiture, this category had sales of $84 million in the U.S. Pfizer's Desitin and J&J's Balmex were two of the three leading diaper rash treatments, with a combined share of nearly 50%. All assets related to Balmex were divested to Chattem.

Diarrhea Remedies

The FTC did not allege the transaction would reduce competition in the diarrhea remedies category. Nonetheless, prior to issuance of the FTC's complaint the parties agreed to divest the Kaopectate brand to Chattem to facilitate FTC clearance of the transaction.[13] At the

---

[13] "Chattem Shares Jump Amid Deal to Acquire J&J, Pfizer Brands," Wall Street Journal, October 6, 2006.

time of the transaction, J&J's Imodium was the leading brand in the category, while Pfizer's Kaopectate had a much smaller share.[14]

Oral Rinses

The FTC did not allege the transaction would reduce competition in the oral rinse category. Nonetheless, prior to issuance of the FTC's complaint the parties agreed to divest the ACT brand to Chattem to facilitate FTC clearance of the transaction.[15] At the time of the transaction, Pfizer's Listerine was the leading brand in the oral rinse category, while J&J's ACT had a much smaller share.[16]

IV.   Data

We utilize retail scanner data collected by ACNielsen for the six product categories containing a divested brand (H2-blockers, hydrocortisones, sleep aids, diaper rash treatments, diarrhea remedies, and oral rinses). This data covers sales in the United States across the food, drug, and mass merchant channels of trade. Three years of weekly data is available, starting in September 2005 (69 weeks pre-divestiture, 87 weeks post-divestiture). Table 1 reports dollar shares for the brands in each category. All brands with at least a 1% share are reported in the table.

For each UPC, the dataset reports dollar and unit sales.[17] In the empirical analysis, we aggregate the data by brand since entire brands were divested rather than individual products (see

---

[14] Since this category was not part of the consent order, the FTC's "Aid to Public Comment" does not report market share and sales information for diarrhea remedies. ACNielsen retail scanner data for the food, drug, and mass merchant channels of trade indicate total category sales of $172 million in 2006, with Imodium and Kaopectate having shares of 68% and 6%, respectively.

[15] See citation in footnote 13.

[16] ACNielsen retail scanner data for the food, drug, and mass merchant channels of trade indicate total category sales of $647 million in 2006, with Listerine and ACT having shares of 52% and 6%, respectively.

[17] The consumer price index is used to convert from nominal to real dollars.

Section V). The aggregation of sales volume for the diarrhea remedies category is complicated

by the fact that each brand's product line contains items with two different units of measure: pill

and liquid forms. We avoid aggregating products with distinct measurement units by estimating

a separate post-divestiture sales change for each brand-form combination. This is not an issue

for the other product categories, where each brand's entire product line is the same form.

The dataset also reports the fraction of stores that carry each UPC. Recognizing that

stores significantly vary by size, ACNielsen weights each store by its annual dollar sales (across

all product categories) when calculating the percentage of stores where a product is available.

This measure is known as "All Commodity Volume" (ACV), and is the standard metric that

brand managers and other practitioners use to quantify a product's retail distribution (Tenn and

Yun, 2008). Each brand's retail distribution is measured by its "Total Distribution Points"

(TDP), which is the sum of its products' ACV. TDP measures the average number of a brand's

products carried per store.[18]

V. Methodology

This section details the approach used to analyze the impact of the J&J – Pfizer

divestitures. Separately for each brand, we estimate the post-divestiture sales change using the

following regression framework.

(1) $\ln r_{bt} = \alpha_b A_t + X_{bt}\beta_b + \varepsilon_{bt}$

Variable r_{bt} denotes brand b's dollar sales in week t, A_t is an indicator variable for the post-

divestiture period, and X_{bt} is a set of additional control variables. These controls consist of

calendar month dummy variables that account for seasonality and, in some specifications, either

a linear time trend or an indicator variable for a transition window between the pre- and post-

---

[18] For example, suppose a brand consists of two UPCs that are available in 50% and 60% of stores,
respectively. The brand's distribution is an average of 1.1 UPCs per store.

divestiture periods (as discussed below). The model is estimated by ordinary least squares.[19] An estimate of each brand's percentage sales change is obtained via the transformation $\alpha_b^* = e^{\alpha_b} - 1$.

Each brand's post-divestiture change in dollar sales is potentially the result of variation in price, sales volume (quantity), and retail distribution (UPCs per store). We consider how these components changed post-divestiture by estimating equation (1) using each of these measures as the dependent variable (in place of dollar sales r_{bt}). One minor complication is that price per unit of measure (ounce or pill) typically varies by package size. Changes in the relative frequency that each package size is purchased can lead to variation in each brand's average price per ounce (or pill) even if all prices remain fixed. To isolate intra-product price variation, we employ a Laspeyres price index, where each UPC's log price is weighed by its dollar sales in the pre-divestiture period.[20]

Equation (1) identifies the post-divestiture sales change by comparing the entire period prior to the divestiture to the entire period afterwards. We also consider a modified specification that allows for a transition period. Transition periods are commonly employed in event studies for two primary reasons. First, firms may behave differently in anticipation of an event occurring. Second, the impact of a given event may be delayed. For example, it can take time for a company to expand its distribution network. As such, divestiture effects may not be immediately apparent. For these reasons, it is common in event studies to employ a transition period that covers the time prior to and following a given event.

---

[19] To account for both heteroscedasticity and autocorrelation, Newey-West standard errors are reported using a lag length of 8 weeks.

[20] As a robustness check, we also estimated the price model using UPC-level data with equation (1) modified to include a set of UPC fixed effects. Similar results were obtained. Note that it is preferable *not* to isolate intra-product variation in the other sales measures. When the model is estimated at the UPC-level, the post-divestiture sales change for each brand is identified solely by products available in both the pre- and post-divestiture periods. Products introduced post-divestiture therefore would not identify the post-divestiture sales change if the model were estimated at the UPC-level. This is problematic since the introduction of new items generally cannibalizes the sales of a brand's existing product line (Reddy et al., 1994). This leads to downward biased estimates of the post-divestiture sales change when the model is estimated at the UPC-level. Such bias does not arise when the model is estimated at the brand-level.

In some specifications, we employ the following transition window. To account for the possibility that the merging parties altered their behavior during the pendency of the transaction, the transition window includes the period between when the J&J – Pfizer transaction was announced and when the divestitures took place (approximately six months later). In addition, the transition window includes the six-month period following the divestitures. We select this length of time based on how long it takes a brand's retail distribution to adjust. Typically, retailers significantly alter the set of products they carry only every six months, during what is known as a "planogram reset" (Cooper and Grutzner, 2008). By including the six-month period following the divestiture within the transition window, our analysis provides sufficient time for any post-divestiture change in retail distribution.[21]

As a second sensitivity check, in some specifications we include a linear time trend in the set of control variables. Accounting for time trends is a challenge in event studies where the effect of interest is identified solely via intertemporal variation. If one controls for the time trend in a very flexible manner then the set of time controls will be highly collinear with the post-divestiture dummy variable, leading to large standard errors. The divestiture effect is not even identified when the time trend is controlled for in the most flexible manner possible: a set of time fixed effects. However, if one controls for the time trend too inflexibly there is a risk that unrelated intertemporal factors may be incorrectly attributed to the divestiture effect. We assess the sensitivity of our results to whether a linear time trend is included in the model specification.

The above framework details a standard "before-after" estimation method. In addition, we consider a "difference in difference" estimator. The post-divestiture change of each divested brand is compared to the counterpart change for a control group. Ideally, the control group should have experienced a change similar to what the divested brand would have experienced in

---

[21] One limitation of using this transition window is that the "before" period is less than a full year (41 weeks). As a robustness check, we considered an alternative specification in which the "before," "transition," and "after" windows correspond to the first, second, and third year of data, respectively. Similar results were obtained. In addition, we considered a shorter transition window corresponding to three months before and after the divestiture. The results are similar to when a transition window is not employed.

the absence of the divestiture. The control group should not only face similar demand and cost shocks, but also be similarly impacted by these shocks (Simpson and Schmidt, 2008).

A second requirement for the control group is that it have a sufficient number of members to account for random variation in each brands' post-divestiture change that is unrelated to the divestiture itself. Donald and Lang (2007) and Tenn (2008) demonstrate this is not possible using a control group consisting of a single entity, since no degrees of freedom remain to estimate the variance of the random component of the post-divestiture change.[22] Research that employs a control group consisting of a single entity has overcome this obstacle by assuming there is no random variation (i.e., the entire difference in the post-divestiture change between the divested brand and the control group brand is attributed to the divestiture). As seen in the results reported in Section VI, the required assumption of no random variation in the post-divestiture change across brands poorly depicts differentiated consumer goods. Violation of this assumption leads to downward biased standard errors since the actual variance of the random component is larger than the maintained assumption of zero variance. Consequently, in the absence of any divestiture impact, one will find a statistically significant effect at, say, the 5% level far more often than 5% of the time.

Construction of a control group that meets the requirements detailed above is clearly a challenge for differentiated consumer products. We use a control group consisting of all brands in the same category with at least a 5% sales share (where private label is treated as a "brand"). This eliminates smaller brands that may not be comparable to the brands divested in the J&J – Pfizer transaction. At the same time, the control group has a sufficient number of members to account for random variation in each brand's post-divestiture change. Depending on the divested product, the control group consists of between two and five brands.[23]

---

[22] Donald and Lang (2007) note it may be possible to obtain information from outside the data sample that could be used to estimate this variance.

[23] See Table 1 for a list of all brands with at least a 1% category share. The imposition of a 5% cutoff eliminates relatively few of these brands.

Using a control group of similar brands in the same category may lead to biased estimates of the post-divestiture change if the control group reacts to any divestiture effect. For example, if the divestiture leads to higher prices, then substitute products may respond by raising price as well. While such bias is a concern, it is not a fatal shortcoming since it does not invalidate testing of whether the divestiture had an effect. Under the null hypothesis that divestitures have no effect when i) market concentration does not change; and ii) the acquirer has significant experience in related product categories, then other brands in the category are a valid control group with which to test that hypothesis (subject to them being sufficiently similar to the divested brand, as detailed above).[24]

We obtain the difference in difference estimates using a two-step method that has previously been used in antitrust analysis to estimate the impact of consummated mergers (e.g., Tenn, 2008; Thompson, 2009).[25] First, equation (1) is separately estimated for each member of the control group. We then use each brand's estimated post-divestiture percentage change $\hat{\alpha}_b^*$ to test whether the change for the divested brand is sufficiently unusual, relative to the control group, that it can reasonably be attributed to the divestiture. To account for inter-brand heterogeneity, we calculate standard errors based on the empirical distribution of the post-divestiture change for the control group. This is accomplished by estimating the following regression model, where the dependent variable is the estimate $\hat{\alpha}_b^*$ obtained above, and D_b is a dummy variable for the divested brand.[26]

(2) $\qquad \hat{\alpha}_b^* = \gamma + \delta D_b + \mu_b$

Parameter δ represents the difference in difference estimator of interest.

---

[24] A divestiture reaction by the control group could, of course, affect the statistical power of this hypothesis test (either positively or negatively, depending on the direction of the reaction).

[25] Donald and Lang (2007) detail the advantages of using a two-stage estimator.

[26] Since the dependent variable in equation (2) is estimated, rather than directly observed, estimation error from the first stage regression (equation (1)) leads to a heteroscedastic error term. We calculate robust standard errors that account for this (Greene, 1997).

Equation (2) is estimated separately for each product category. Note that the number of observations included in the regression equals the number of control group members plus one (the divested brand). This highlights a potential difficulty in identifying divestiture effects; the small size of our control group leads to relatively imprecise estimates of the difference in difference estimator δ. This is particularly true for product categories with significant inter-brand heterogeneity in the post-divestiture change (i.e., the variance of μ in equation (2) is large).

VI.   Results

Table 2 presents the post-divestiture change for each divested brand. In this baseline specification, we do not control for a time trend or employ a transition window. The results indicate the price of every divested brand declined post-divestiture. The price reduction is relatively small for all of the divested brands except for Kaopectate pill form, which reduced price by 38% (as discussed below, this is due to a product line discontinuation unrelated to the divestiture).

There is much more diversity in the post-divestiture change in sales. Three of the brands underwent relatively little change: Zantac (H2-blocker), Cortizone (hydrocortisone), and Unisom (sleep aid). Depending on the dependent variable employed (dollar sales, sales volume, or retail distribution), these brands either did not significantly change post-divestiture, or slightly increased. In contrast, two of the brands, Balmex (diaper rash treatment) and Kaopectate (diarrhea remedy), underwent a significant sales reduction, while ACT (oral rinse) substantially increased sales.[27]

---

[27] Of these three brands, only Balmex was part of the J&J – Pfizer consent agreement with the FTC. Although Kaopectate and ACT were divested in anticipation of possible antitrust concern, the FTC did not allege the proposed transaction would have anticompetitive effects in either the oral rinse or diarrhea remedies categories.

For the three brands that experienced a major post-divestiture sales change, these changes are largely due to variation in retail distribution unrelated to the divestiture.[28] Kaopectate's decline is due to the discontinuation of its line of pills (Kaopectate is primarily sold in liquid form). While this product line was discontinued by Pfizer prior to the divestiture, this process took a long time to complete as retailers sold their existing inventory. See Figure 1.

ACT's distribution increase is due to product introductions: two new flavors, and a larger bottle size. All of these new products were introduced pre-divestiture, but the expansion process extended into the post-divestiture period as retailers slowly added the new products to their store shelves. See Figure 2.

The likely explanation for Balmex's reduction in retail distribution is the rapid expansion of several small brands of diaper rash treatment (these brands increased distribution by 56% to 188%, see Table 2). The additional shelf space these brands obtained came, in part, at the expense of Balmex (the remaining distribution increase came from category expansion). Of the three major brands of diaper rash treatment, Balmex had the smallest market share and the lowest average sales per distribution point. These may have been contributing factors for why the expanding fringe brands displaced Balmex (rather than category leaders Desitin and A+D). It is important to note that the growth of the smaller diaper rash brands, and the decline of Balmex, started substantially prior to the divestiture and continued the entire period covered by the data. See Figure 3.

To summarize, the results from our baseline specification indicate that i) the price of every divested brand fell; and ii) three of the brands performed as well or slightly better post-divestiture, while the much larger sales changes experienced by the remaining three brands do

---

[28] As a robustness check, we estimated the model using dollar and volume sales per distribution point as the dependent variable. For Balmex, these results show that its post-divestiture sales change is almost entirely due to a loss in retail distribution. ACT's dollar sales per distribution point fell by approximately 10%, although its volume sales per distribution point fell only slightly. This difference is due to the introduction of a larger bottle size that had a lower price per ounce than ACT's existing product line. Kaopectate experienced a major decline in both dollar and volume sales per distribution point. As discussed below, this is the result of a product line discontinuation.

not appear to be divestiture-related. These results provide a good sense of how each brand's performance changed post-divestiture. From an antitrust policy perspective, however, the key issue is how the divested brands performed relative to what would have occurred but-for the divestitures. This is a much more difficult problem, and requires an assumption regarding each brand's counterfactual performance had the divestitures not taken place. The results reported above represent the impact of the divestitures only if one assumes that each brand's post-divestiture change is entirely due to the divestiture itself.

An alternative way to construct each brand's post-divestiture counterfactual is to assume that each brand's pre-divestiture sales trend would have continued but-for the divestiture. We implement this assumption by controlling for a linear time trend. The post-divesture effect is measured as the deviation from the divested brand's trend. As discussed in Section V, as a second robustness check we also explore the impact of using a transition window.

The results of these sensitivity analyses are presented in Table 3, which reports alternative specifications that differ with respect to whether a linear time trend or a transition window is employed.[29] To aid comparison, the first specification reported in the table corresponds to the baseline model presented earlier in Table 2. Very few results are robust across the specifications presented in Table 3, with "no change" usually lying within the range of estimates. In only two instances are the point estimates from all of the specifications the same sign and statistically significant at the 5% level; Kaopectate pill and liquid forms both had a post-divestiture decline in retail distribution. As discussed above, the decline in the Kaopectate pill product line is due to its discontinuation, rather than being a divestiture effect. It is also unlikely that the decline in Kaopectate liquid form is the result of the divestiture since, as discussed

---

[29] The results from a specification that includes both a time trend and a transition window are very sensitive to changes in the model specification (e.g., the alternative transition windows discussed in footnote 21). This is not surprising given that the post-divestiture and transition window dummy variables and the linear time trend all vary only as a function of time, which makes it difficult to identify the divestiture impact. Due to their unreliability, we do not report results from this specification.

below, this decline is similar to the post-divestiture change for other major brands in the diarrhea remedies category.

Another potential comparison is to analyze the post-divestiture change of the divested brand relative to the post-divestiture change for a control group. As discussed in Section V, the control group consists of all other brands in the category with at least a 5% sales share. A difficulty with this approach is that each control group contains a limited number of relatively heterogeneous brands. Control group heterogeneity makes it difficult to test whether the post-divestiture change of the divested brand is sufficiently unusual that it can reasonably be attributed to the divestiture.

Table 4 presents the "difference in difference" results. The estimates are generally quite imprecise.[30] The only estimates that are statistically significant at the 5% level are the results for Kaopectate pill form, which in some specifications experienced a statistically significant decline in dollar and volume sales, retail distribution, and price. As detailed above, however, this is not likely a result of the divestiture (but, rather, a product line discontinuation).

VII.   Conclusion

This study analyzes the performance of the brands divested in the J&J – Pfizer transaction. The results from a standard "before-after" estimator show the price of every divested brand fell post-divestiture (albeit only slightly in most cases). The divested brands performed as well or better in the post-divestiture period, or underwent major changes that do not appear to be divestiture related.

These results reveal how each brand's performance changed post-divestiture. From a policy perspective, however, the key issue is how the divested brands performed relative to what

---

[30] Large standard errors are a direct result of accounting for heterogeneity across the control group brands. Ignoring random variation in each brand's post-divestiture change leads to substantially smaller standard errors, with a large number of statistically significant effects (both positive and negative). This highlights the risk of incorrect inference in studies that ignore random variation in each brand's performance (Donald and Lang, 2007).

would have occurred but-for the J&J – Pfizer transaction. We find the results are quite sensitive to the maintained assumption regarding the divested brands' counterfactual performance. A consistent finding, however, is that "no change" lies within the range of estimates obtained under various modeling assumptions.

We also consider a "difference in difference" estimator that measures the post-divestiture change relative to a control group. The results from this analysis do not reveal a statistically significant divestiture impact. However, substantial heterogeneity across the control group leads to imprecise estimates, diminishing the statistical power of this test.

The results indicate the post-divestiture performance of the divested brands is similar to their pre-divestiture performance. This suggests the divestitures maintained the pre-transaction level of competition. However, uncertainty regarding the divested brands' counterfactual performance makes it impossible to determine whether the divestitures maintained the competitive environment that would have occurred in the absence of the J&J – Pfizer transaction. If one starts with the prior that divestitures should have little impact when i) market concentration does not change; and ii) the acquirer has significant experience in related product categories, then our overall results are consistent with that hypothesis (i.e., we cannot reject the null). Admittedly, this is weaker than concluding the divestitures had no effect.

Our analysis highlights the inherent difficulty of conducting retrospective studies to determine the success of antitrust policy. While typically it is possible to determine what happened following a divestiture or a merger, it is far more difficult to conclude whether the observed change can reasonably be attributed to the analyzed event. We believe retrospective analyses of antitrust policy are useful, and more should be undertaken in the future. Nonetheless, it is important to recognize the limitations of such analyses and to consider carefully the sensitivity of the obtained results to different modeling assumptions.

References

Ashenfelter, Orley, and Daniel Hosken. 2008. "The Effect of Mergers on Consumer Prices: Evidence from Five Selected Case Studies," NBER Working Paper No. 13859.

Baer, William J., and Ronald C. Redcay. 2001. "Solving Competition Problems in Merger Control: The Requirements for an Effective Divestiture Remedy," *George Washington Law Review* 69(5/6): 915-931.

Breen, Denis A. 2004. "The Union Pacific/Southern Pacific Rail Merger: A Retrospective on Merger Benefits," *Review of Network Economics* 3(3): 283-322.

Burke, Jim. 1998. "Divestiture as an Antitrust Remedy in Bank Mergers," Federal Reserve FEDS Working Paper No. 1998-14.

Cooper, Scott W., and Fritz P. Grutzner. 2008. *Tips and Traps for Marketing Your Business.* McGraw-Hill.

Cotterill, Ronald W., Tirtha P. Dhar, and Andrew W. Franklin. 1999. "Post Merger Price Conduct: A Case Study of Pricing in Connecticut Markets After the 1996 Royal Ahold-Stop & Shop Merger," Food Marketing Policy Center Research Report No. 47.

Donald, Stephen G., and Kevin Lang. 2007. "Inference with Difference-in-Differences and Other Panel Data," *Review of Economics and Statistics* 89(2): 221-233.

Elzinga, Kenneth G. 1969. "The Antimerger Law: Pyrrhic Victories?," *Journal of Law and Economics* 12(1): 43-78.

Federal Trade Commission, Bureau of Competition. 1999. *A Study of the Commission's Divestiture Process.*

Greene, William H. 1997. *Econometric Analysis*, 3rd Edition. Prentice Hall.

Haas-Wilson, Deborah, and Christopher Garmon. 2009. "Two Hospital Mergers on Chicago's North Shore: A Retrospective Study," FTC Bureau of Economics Working Paper No. 294.

Hastings, Justine S., and Richard J. Gilbert. 2005. "Market Power, Vertical Integration and the Wholesale Price of Gasoline," *Journal of Industrial Economics* 53(4): 469-492.

Hunter, Graeme, Gregory K. Leonard, and G. Steven Olley. 2008. "Merger Retrospective Studies: A Review," *Antitrust* 23(1): 34-41.

Kaplan, Steven N. (ed.) 2000. *Mergers and Productivity.* NBER Conference Report, University of Chicago Press.

Pautler, Paul A. 2003. "Evidence on Mergers and Acquisitions," *Antitrust Bulletin* 48(1): 119-221.

Pesendorfer, Martin. 2003. "Horizontal Mergers in the Paper Industry," *RAND Journal of Economics* 34(3): 495-515.

Peters, Craig. 2006. "Evaluating the Performance of Merger Simulation: Evidence from the U.S. Airline Industry," *Journal of Law and Economics* 49(2): 627-649.

Piloff, Steven J. 2002. "What's Happened at Divested Bank Offices? An Empirical Analysis of Antitrust Divestitures in Bank Mergers." Federal Reserve FEDS Working Paper No. 2002-60.

Reddy, Srinivas K., Susan L. Holak, and Subodh Bhat. 1994. "To Extend or Not to Extend: Success Determinants of Line Extensions," *Journal of Marketing Research* 31(2): 243-262.

Rogers, Robert P., and Benjamin Hollinger. 2004. "The Impact on Product Prices of Mergers in the Petroleum Industry," *Southwestern Economic Review* 31(1): 57-78.

Rogowsky, Robert A. 1986. "The Economic Effectiveness of Section 7 Relief," *Antitrust Bulletin* 31(3):187-233.

Simpson, John, and David Schmidt. 2008. "Difference-in-Differences Analysis in Antitrust: A Cautionary Note," *Antitrust Law Journal* 75(2): 623-636.

Simpson, John, and Christopher Taylor. 2008. "Do Gasoline Mergers Affect Consumer Prices? The Marathon Ashland Petroleum and Ultramar Diamond Shamrock Transaction," *Journal of Law and Economics* 51(1): 135-152.

Soetevent, Adriaan R., Marco A. Haan, and Pim Heijnen. 2008. "Do Auctions and Forced Divestitures Increase Competition?," Tinbergen Institute Discussion Paper No. TI 2008-117/1.

Tenn, Steven. 2008. "The Price Effects of Hospital Mergers: A Case Study of the Sutter-Summit Transaction," FTC Bureau of Economics Working Paper No. 293.

Tenn, Steven, and John M. Yun. 2008. "Biases in Demand Analysis Due to Variation in Retail Distribution," *International Journal of Industrial Organization* 26(4): 984-997.

Thompson, Aileen. 2009. "The Effect of Hospital Mergers on Inpatient Prices: A Case Study of the New Hanover-Cape Fear Transaction," FTC Bureau of Economics Working Paper No. 295.

United States General Accounting Office. 2002. "Federal Trade Commission: Study Needed to Assess the Effects of Recent Divestitures on Competition in Retail Markets." GAO-02-793.

Vita, Michael G., and Seth Sacher. 2001. "The Competitive Effects of Not-for-Profit Hospital Mergers: A Case Study," *Journal of Industrial Economics* 49(1): 63-84.

Weinberg, Matthew. 2008. "The Price Effects of Horizontal Mergers," *Journal of Competition Law and Economics* 4(2): 433-447.

Whinston, Michael D. 2006. *Lectures on Antitrust Economics*, Chapter 3. MIT Press.

Table 1: Category Dollar Share by Brand

H2-Blockers

Brand	Share
PEPCID	39%
ZANTAC	33%
PRIVATE LABEL	22%
TAGAMET	4%

Hydrocortisones

Brand	Share
PRIVATE LABEL	37%
CORTIZONE	34%
CORTAID	17%
AVEENO	4%
SOOTHING CARE	2%
SUNMARK	1%

Sleep Aids

Brand	Share
PRIVATE LABEL	31%
UNISOM	25%
SIMPLY SLEEP	22%
SOMINEX	6%
IOVATE SLEEP	4%
SLEEPINAL	3%
MID NITE	2%
HYLANDS	2%
NYTOL	1%

Diaper Rash Treatments

Brand	Share
DESITIN	34%
A+D	23%
BALMEX	11%
BOUDREAUX	9%
PRIVATE LABEL	8%
TRIPLE PASTE	6%
AVEENO	3%
DR. SMITH'S	2%

Diarrhea Remedies

Brand	Share
IMODIUM	68%
PRIVATE LABEL	23%
KAOPECTATE	6%
FLORASTOR	1%

Oral Rinses

Brand	Share
LISTERINE	51%
PRIVATE LABEL	13%
CREST	11%
SCOPE	8%
ACT	6%
BIOTENE	2%
COLGATE	2%
PLAX	1%

Notes: Calculations based on ACNielsen retail scanner data for the food, drug, and mass merchant channels of trade for the period September 11, 2005, to September 6, 2008. The table contains all brands with at least a 1% category share. The divested brand in each category is highlighted.

Table 2: Post-Divestiture Changes by Brand, Baseline Model

A. H2-Blockers

Brand	Form	Share	Dollar Sales	Sales Volume	Distribution	Price
PEPCID	CT	39%	-14.1% (1.4%)	-14.2% (1.1%)	-16.4% (1.6%)	0.1% (1.8%)
ZANTAC	CT	33%	0.4% (2.2%)	2.1% (1.7%)	7.8% (2.2%)	-1.9% (0.7%)
PRIVATE LABEL	CT	22%	11.2% (1.4%)	8.8% (1.3%)	14.0% (2.1%)	-1.5% (0.6%)

B. Hydrocortisones

Brand	Form	Share	Dollar Sales	Sales Volume	Distribution	Price
PRIVATE LABEL	OZ	37%	2.2% (1.0%)	1.6% (1.0%)	5.8% (0.7%)	0.2% (0.7%)
CORTIZONE	OZ	34%	2.0% (2.3%)	4.1% (2.4%)	2.9% (1.9%)	-4.7% (0.5%)
CORTAID	OZ	17%	-17.6% (3.3%)	-21.1% (3.0%)	-11.4% (2.5%)	-5.9% (0.6%)

C. Sleep Aids

Brand	Form	Share	Dollar Sales	Sales Volume	Distribution	Price
PRIVATE LABEL	CT	31%	14.6% (1.5%)	22.4% (2.3%)	15.3% (1.9%)	-2.9% (0.6%)
UNISOM	CT	25%	0.0% (2.4%)	4.3% (2.6%)	3.2% (2.1%)	-3.5% (0.6%)
SIMPLY SLEEP	CT	22%	0.5% (1.9%)	6.4% (1.4%)	-0.7% (0.8%)	-2.4% (0.9%)
SOMINEX	CT	6%	-11.6% (2.4%)	-12.5% (2.6%)	-10.5% (1.8%)	0.7% (0.8%)

D. Diaper Rash Treatments

Brand	Form	Share	Dollar Sales	Sales Volume	Distribution	Price
DESITIN	OZ	34%	-0.1% (0.9%)	2.9% (0.7%)	6.1% (0.8%)	-2.2% (1.2%)
A+D	OZ	23%	-5.4% (1.1%)	3.7% (1.1%)	4.1% (0.8%)	-5.8% (0.8%)
BALMEX	OZ	11%	-19.6% (2.5%)	-15.3% (2.2%)	-17.5% (1.8%)	-5.2% (1.1%)
BOUDREAUX	OZ	9%	23.6% (4.1%)	35.7% (6.3%)	56.1% (9.8%)	-3.2% (0.7%)
PRIVATE LABEL	OZ	8%	22.6% (1.7%)	25.4% (2.3%)	31.7% (4.2%)	0.2% (1.0%)
TRIPLE PASTE	OZ	6%	68.3% (8.1%)	105.4% (12.9%)	188.3% (25.3%)	-4.9% (0.5%)

E. Diarrhea Remedies

Brand	Form	Share	Dollar Sales	Sales Volume	Distribution	Price
IMODIUM	CT	59%	-0.8% (1.7%)	4.0% (1.6%)	-0.9% (1.1%)	-2.0% (0.8%)
	OZ	8%	-16.6% (1.8%)	-19.6% (1.9%)	-13.5% (1.4%)	-1.4% (0.5%)
PRIVATE LABEL	CT	22%	1.5% (1.5%)	5.2% (1.4%)	5.2% (1.2%)	-1.4% (0.6%)
	OZ	1%	-30.6% (3.4%)	-39.2% (4.5%)	-21.7% (3.2%)	-8.9% (1.3%)
KAOPECTATE	OZ	5%	-5.7% (1.9%)	-1.9% (2.2%)	-5.0% (1.7%)	-3.5% (0.5%)
	CT	1%	-98.4% (0.8%)	-97.8% (1.0%)	-94.0% (1.2%)	-38.3% (4.6%)

F. Oral Rinses

Brand	Form	Share	Dollar Sales	Sales Volume	Distribution	Price
LISTERINE	OZ	51%	-0.4% (1.4%)	3.2% (1.2%)	9.8% (2.5%)	-4.0% (0.6%)
PRIVATE LABEL	OZ	13%	6.2% (1.4%)	5.1% (1.4%)	3.4% (1.1%)	0.5% (0.9%)
CREST	OZ	11%	44.3% (6.0%)	39.1% (5.2%)	53.1% (9.6%)	0.8% (0.5%)
SCOPE	OZ	8%	-11.7% (1.8%)	-12.5% (1.9%)	-15.6% (2.1%)	-4.1% (0.5%)
ACT	OZ	6%	18.8% (3.5%)	27.8% (4.5%)	32.3% (3.7%)	-2.0% (0.5%)

Notes: Newey-West standard errors are reported in parentheses. The divested brand in each category is highlighted. Measurement units: OZ = ounce, CT = count.

Table 3: Post-Divestiture Changes by Brand, Sensitivity Analyses

A. H2-Blockers

Brand	Form	Transition Window?	Time Trend?	Dollar Sales	Sales Volume	Distribution	Price
ZANTAC	CT	N	N	0.4% (2.2%)	2.1% (1.7%)	7.8% (2.2%)	-1.9% (0.7%)
		Y	N	2.0% (2.7%)	4.8% (1.9%)	12.3% (2.1%)	-2.1% (0.7%)
		N	Y	4.8% (5.3%)	0.6% (4.0%)	-0.3% (2.8%)	1.0% (1.4%)

B. Hydrocortisones

Brand	Form	Transition Window?	Time Trend?	Dollar Sales	Sales Volume	Distribution	Price
CORTIZONE	OZ	N	N	2.0% (2.3%)	4.1% (2.4%)	2.9% (1.9%)	-4.7% (0.5%)
		Y	N	1.6% (2.9%)	4.9% (2.8%)	4.2% (2.1%)	-6.1% (0.5%)
		N	Y	-2.9% (3.6%)	-4.0% (3.8%)	-6.8% (2.9%)	-0.6% (0.7%)

C. Sleep Aids

Brand	Form	Transition Window?	Time Trend?	Dollar Sales	Sales Volume	Distribution	Price
UNISOM	CT	N	N	0.0% (2.4%)	4.3% (2.6%)	3.2% (2.1%)	-3.5% (0.6%)
		Y	N	-4.1% (2.6%)	1.2% (3.2%)	1.3% (2.4%)	-4.6% (0.4%)
		N	Y	11.6% (4.0%)	9.9% (4.3%)	3.9% (3.8%)	0.9% (1.0%)

D. Diaper Rash Treatments

Brand	Form	Transition Window?	Time Trend?	Dollar Sales	Sales Volume	Distribution	Price
BALMEX	OZ	N	N	-19.6% (2.5%)	-15.3% (2.2%)	-17.5% (1.8%)	-5.2% (1.1%)
		Y	N	-23.9% (2.5%)	-18.4% (2.4%)	-22.4% (1.4%)	-6.2% (0.9%)
		N	Y	-2.4% (4.5%)	-2.6% (3.8%)	-1.7% (1.9%)	0.2% (2.6%)

E. Diarrhea Remedies

Brand	Form	Transition Window?	Time Trend?	Dollar Sales	Sales Volume	Distribution	Price
KAOPECTATE	OZ	N	N	-5.7% (1.9%)	-1.9% (2.2%)	-5.0% (1.7%)	-3.5% (0.5%)
		Y	N	-6.8% (2.4%)	-1.3% (2.6%)	-5.0% (1.9%)	-4.6% (0.3%)
		N	Y	-6.3% (4.3%)	-8.0% (4.6%)	-8.4% (3.8%)	-0.2% (0.8%)
KAOPECTATE	CT	N	N	-98.4% (0.8%)	-97.8% (1.0%)	-94.0% (1.2%)	-38.3% (4.6%)
		Y	N	-99.6% (0.1%)	-99.4% (0.2%)	-97.0% (0.6%)	-48.2% (2.8%)
		N	Y	16.2% (83.4%)	-2.2% (63.8%)	-73.2% (8.0%)	12.9% (12.4%)

F. Oral Rinses

Brand	Form	Transition Window?	Time Trend?	Dollar Sales	Sales Volume	Distribution	Price
ACT	OZ	N	N	18.8% (3.5%)	27.8% (4.5%)	32.3% (3.7%)	-2.0% (0.5%)
		Y	N	26.6% (3.6%)	38.5% (4.3%)	43.9% (2.4%)	-2.9% (0.6%)
		N	Y	-3.8% (4.4%)	-1.8% (5.5%)	5.1% (3.2%)	-0.8% (1.0%)

Notes: Newey-West standard errors are reported in parentheses. Measurement units: OZ = ounce, CT = count.

Table 4: Post-Divestiture Changes by Brand, Difference in Difference Estimates

A. H2-Blockers

Brand	Form	Transition Window?	Time Trend?	Dollar Sales	Sales Volume	Distribution	Price
ZANTAC	CT	N	N	1.9% (21.9%)	4.8% (20.0%)	9.0% (26.3%)	-1.2% (1.2%)
		Y	N	3.3% (27.9%)	7.7% (26.0%)	13.0% (36.3%)	-2.1% (3.7%)
		N	Y	5.1% (5.6%)	4.1% (6.2%)	4.4% (3.6%)	0.8% (2.6%)

B. Hydrocortisones

Brand	Form	Transition Window?	Time Trend?	Dollar Sales	Sales Volume	Distribution	Price
CORTIZONE	OZ	N	N	9.7% (17.2%)	13.8% (19.7%)	5.8% (14.9%)	-1.8% (5.3%)
		Y	N	11.6% (22.9%)	18.1% (25.8%)	7.3% (19.0%)	-3.0% (8.0%)
		N	Y	-5.8% (6.3%)	-6.1% (4.5%)	-8.5% (3.4%)	1.4% (1.1%)

C. Sleep Aids

Brand	Form	Transition Window?	Time Trend?	Dollar Sales	Sales Volume	Distribution	Price
UNISOM	CT	N	N	-1.2% (15.2%)	-1.1% (20.2%)	1.9% (15.1%)	-2.0% (2.2%)
		Y	N	-5.6% (20.8%)	-6.2% (27.4%)	-0.3% (20.5%)	-2.8% (2.9%)
		N	Y	5.2% (4.6%)	3.9% (4.7%)	0.7% (4.0%)	0.1% (2.4%)

D. Diaper Rash Treatments

Brand	Form	Transition Window?	Time Trend?	Dollar Sales	Sales Volume	Distribution	Price
BALMEX	OZ	N	N	-41.4% (31.8%)	-49.9% (45.7%)	-74.7% (82.9%)	-2.0% (2.6%)
		Y	N	-56.0% (47.7%)	-71.9% (72.0%)	-113.2% (134.4%)	-1.7% (2.8%)
		N	Y	-9.5% (9.4%)	-9.6% (14.1%)	-12.1% (25.8%)	0.5% (4.9%)

E. Diarrhea Remedies

Brand	Form	Transition Window?	Time Trend?	Dollar Sales		Sales Volume		Distribution		Price	
KAOPECTATE	OZ	N	N	5.9% (16.8%)		10.5% (23.7%)		2.8% (13.6%)		-0.1% (3.5%)	
		Y	N	7.6% (20.7%)		13.5% (28.0%)		3.9% (17.0%)		-0.4% (5.7%)	
		N	Y	-1.6% (5.0%)		1.5% (5.4%)		-0.4% (13.0%)		-0.1% (1.2%)	
KAOPECTATE	CT	N	N	-86.8% (16.7%)	*	-85.4% (23.6%)	*	-86.3% (13.5%)	*	-34.9% (5.7%)	*
		Y	N	-85.2% (20.5%)	*	-84.6% (27.9%)		-88.0% (16.9%)	*	-44.0% (6.3%)	*
		N	Y	20.9% (83.4%)		7.3% (63.9%)		-65.2% (14.8%)	*	13.0% (12.4%)	

F. Oral Rinses

Brand	Form	Transition Window?	Time Trend?	Dollar Sales	Sales Volume	Distribution	Price
ACT	OZ	N	N	9.2% (27.2%)	19.1% (24.5%)	19.6% (32.3%)	-0.3% (3.0%)
		Y	N	12.2% (40.8%)	26.0% (37.1%)	21.2% (54.3%)	-0.9% (4.0%)
		N	Y	-7.8% (9.1%)	-5.7% (7.9%)	7.6% (4.2%)	0.0% (1.8%)

Notes: Difference in difference estimates obtained using a two-step method (see Section V for details). Robust standard errors are reported that account for heteroscedasticity from using an estimated dependent variable in the second stage regression. The control group consists of all other brands in the category with at least a 5% share. Statistical significance: *=5%. Measurement units: OZ = ounce, CT = count.

Figure 1: Retail Distribution of Kaopectate Pill Product Line

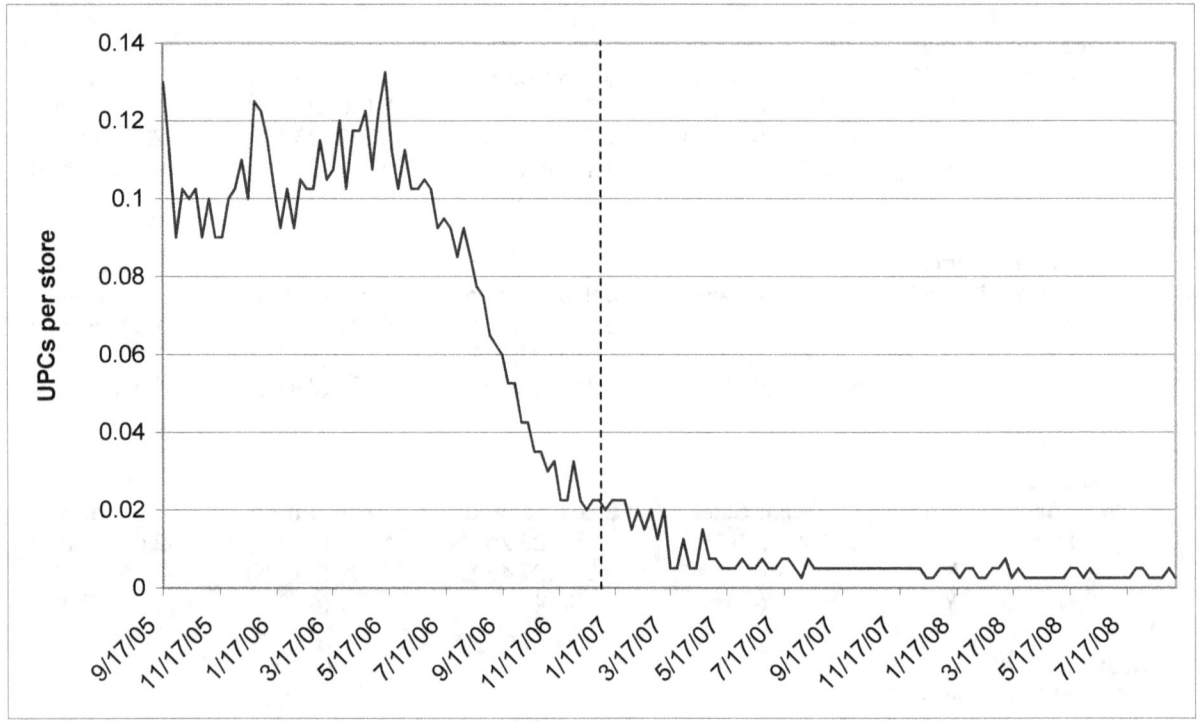

Notes: The vertical line notes the date of the divestiture.

Figure 2: Retail Distribution of ACT

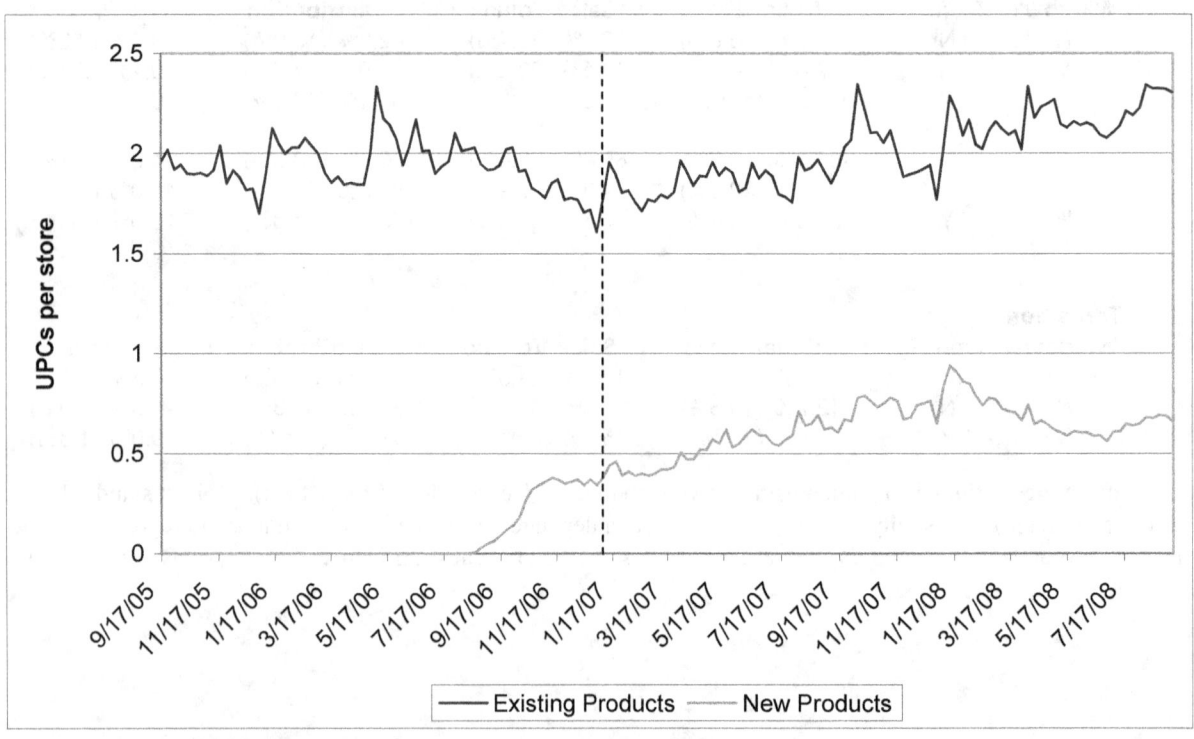

Notes: "New products" consist of the ACT UPCs introduced during the period covered by the data. "Existing products" consist of all other ACT UPCs. The vertical line notes the date of the divestiture.

Figure 3: Retail Distribution of Diaper Rash Treatments

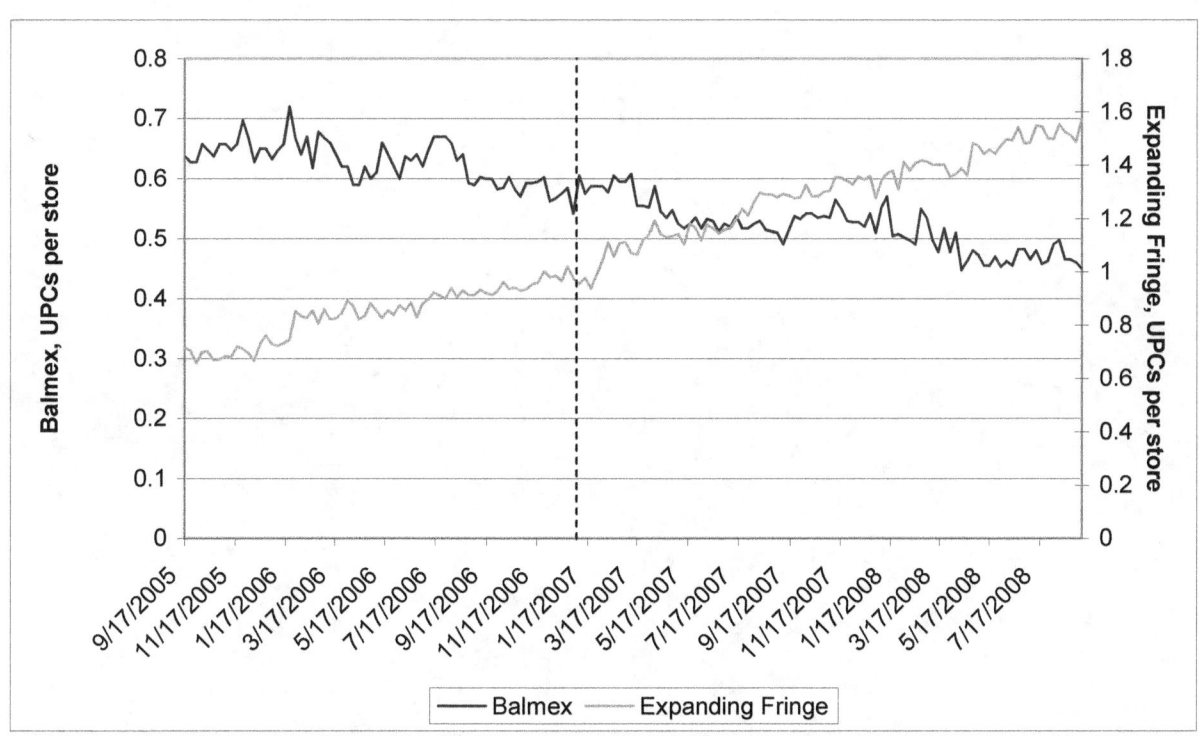

Notes: The "expanding fringe" brands consist of Boudreaux, Triple Paste, and Private Label. The vertical line notes the date of the divestiture.

www.ingramcontent.com/pod-product-compliance
Lightning Source LLC
Chambersburg PA
CBHW081249170526
45165CB00009B/3262